Good Morning, Grandma!

Written by Lisa Trumbauer

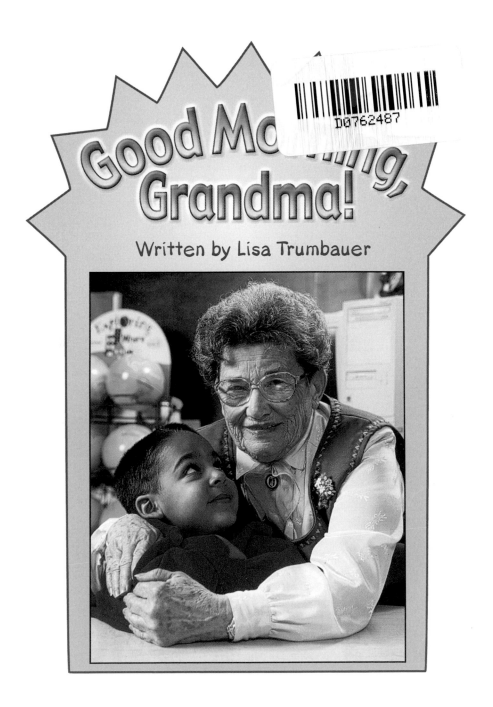

Celebration Press

Parsippany, New Jersey

It's Monday morning. Children everywhere
wake up and get dressed. They eat breakfast
and get their books and homework together.
For most children Monday morning means it's
time to go to school.

This is Phyllis. She is going somewhere on this Monday morning, too. Where is Phyllis going? She's going to school as well!

Phyllis is a member of the Foster
Grandparent Program. Each school day,
she visits classrooms to help students.

She helps by giving children a little bit of extra attention and care.

The Foster Grandparent Program started in 1965. It gives people 60 and older who have time on their hands and love in their hearts a chance to make a real difference in the lives of young children.

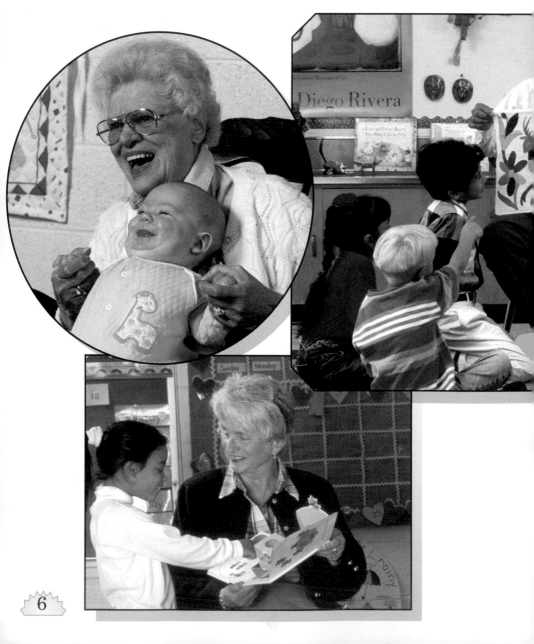

Today you can find Foster Grandparent volunteers in many places, helping lots of children.

Phyllis's day begins in a kindergarten
classroom. Here she works with students in
small groups. These children are part of a
getting-ready-to-read program.

Phyllis helps young children learn the names of colors and letters. She also helps them with coloring and cutting. All these things can be hard to do! Phyllis is patient and kind, and she makes it fun to practice and learn.

Next Phyllis moves on to a fifth-grade class.
She works one-on-one with some of the
students in this classroom. She helps in all
sorts of ways. Most of all, she helps children
feel good about what they can do. Children also
learn not to feel bad about things that are hard
for them. Phyllis is there to help them.

After her fifth-grade class, Phyllis assists in another getting-ready-to-read program. This one is in a pre-first-grade class. Phyllis reinforces what children learned the week before.

This means she reviews with children things that they have already worked on. Sometimes it takes more than one lesson before you get it!

Phyllis's day isn't over yet! After lunch it's on
to another class of older students. Phyllis
works with one student at a time. They work
on whatever seems to be causing trouble.
Sometimes they just talk.

Often she helps students with reading or spelling. They play lots of learning games. "They're always beating me!" Phyllis laughs.

Not every adult can be a Foster Grandparent
volunteer. People must first apply to the
program. They must be 60 years of age or older.

They must also pass a physical examination. Foster Grandparent volunteers need a lot of energy and must be in good health. It takes a healthy and energetic person to work with children!

Then they must pass a special class that explains the sorts of things they might be doing with their "foster grandchildren."

Foster Grandparent volunteers also need one more important thing. They must love children and believe in them. They must want to help them.

That's why Phyllis got involved.

"After my good friend died, I wanted to do something meaningful," says Phyllis. "My neighbor told me about the program. I love children, so I applied.

"I feel wonderful when children learn to cut, color, get 100 on a test, read a story. I helped them do it!"

Phyllis remembers one little girl in kindergarten who would never talk. Every morning Phyllis would tell her good morning, but there was never an answer. So Phyllis would answer for her—"Good morning, Grandma." One morning when Phyllis came in, the girl said, "Good morning, Grandma," in a very soft voice. Phyllis pretended she hadn't understood her, and asked her to say it again, louder.

"Good morning, Grandma!" she said, loud and clear.

"And from then on, she started talking at school," Phyllis remembers. "She was even in a program on stage at the end of the year."

Phyllis and the little girl are still special friends. Sometimes they still work together.

It's been a full day, and Phyllis is a little tired. But she doesn't mind. It's a good kind of tired! Phyllis will be back tomorrow.

"We're such a help for children," she says. "We influence them in the right way. And we show how much we care," Phyllis says. "I love everything about it."

Children seem to love their Foster Grandparents, too!